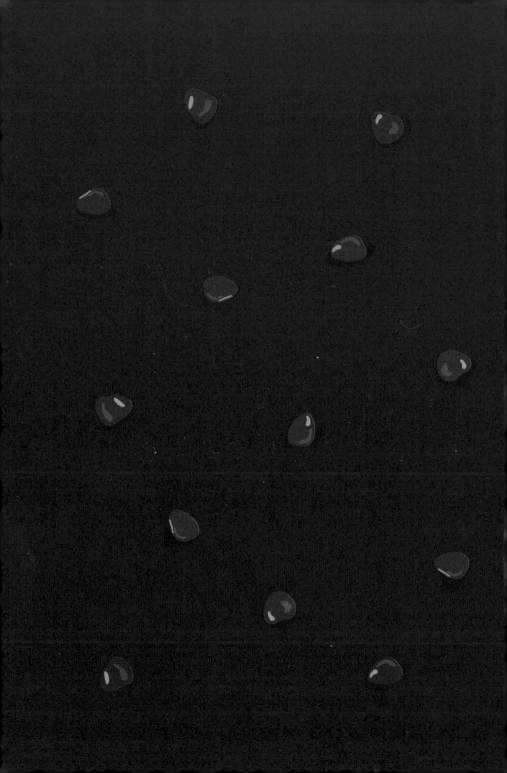

Watermelon Credo™
- The Book -

Aloha

"Be Positive Regardless!"

5-10-11

Wally Amos
with Stu Glauberman

Illustrated by Suzanne Hallerman

Credo Press™

This book is dedicated to watermelon lovers everywhere

Acknowledgments

In keeping with our belief that great teamwork makes for the greatest success, the authors wish to express heartfelt thanks and appreciation to editor Ellen Wheat, illustrator and designer Suzanne Hallerman, and project and prepress manager Susan Dupèrè. Their talent, commitment, dedication, team spirit, and enthusiasm contributed enormously to our work. In most successful endeavors, there is the utility person, the volunteer, who does everything well just as a friend. For this project, and many others, that person is Robert Brooks. Thanks Robert.

– Wally and Stu

Copyright © 2010 by Wally Amos and Stu Glauberman

All rights reserved. No part of this book may be reproduced, stored in a retrieval system, or transmitted in any form or by any means, electronic, mechanical, photocopying, recording, or otherwise, without the written permission of the authors. Permission is given for brief excerpts to be published with reviews in newspapers, magazines, newsletters, catalogs, and online publications.

Illustrations by Suzanne Hallerman
Project and prepress manager: Susan Dupèrè
Editor: Ellen Wheat
Designer: Suzanne Hallerman
Photographs by Dana Edmunds
Consultant: Robert A. Brooks
Wally's watermelon hats, shirts, and shoes
designed by Christine Harris–Amos

Library of Congress Control Number: 2010902321
ISBN 978-0-615-34947-3

First edition, 2010

Credo Press™
PO Box 897
Kailua, HI 96734
tel. 808.261.1811

Printed in China

Contents

Of Cookies and Credos

Simply put, a credo is a belief system.

Long ago, a Crusader might follow his credo into battle or, as *Man of La Mancha* lyricist Joe Darion put it so passionately, "march into hell for a heavenly cause."

In modern times, a hotel company like The Ritz-Carlton uses a credo to motivate employees to embody its philosophy of service excellence.

How did I, Wally Amos, who became famous as a cookie man, come to combine the heavenly magic of watermelon with the mundane business of writing down a belief system as a credo? Hey, that's what I do! I'm the kind of person who likes to connect happy, wonderfully funny things and ideas to a serious purpose that can point people in a better direction and maybe even lift them up like a dirigible to a higher plane.

I'm known as the Cookie Man and it's true, a cookie man I am, I am. I've written several books describing in delicious detail my life in cookies, how for more than 40 years, I've been making and baking and churning out fresh cookies as an expression of love. As much as I like to make cookies for other people and see faces light up with cookie-eating pleasure, I also enjoy eating my cookies.

I love the delectable wholesomeness that's baked into every bite with only the highest quality ingredients. And there's something about devouring freshly baked cookies that makes me feel happy all over and keeps me feeling young. If you're young, you can look forward to years and years of enjoying cookies as you mature, and come to appreciate how truly wonderful it was to have a cookie-filled childhood. But hey! If you're no longer young, don't stop eating cookies, now!

I also love watermelon. I wear hats and shirts and shoes patterned on that scrumptious ruby-red fruit packed into its sleek, smooth, dark-green carrying case. In my 1996 book, *Watermelon Magic: Seeds of Wisdom, Slices of Life*, I wrote a lot of juicy stuff about watermelon. That book is also about making personal choices, empowering yourself to make positive choices based on what you believe, not what others want you to believe.

Not long after that book came out, I was sitting at a book-signing table when it occurred to me that I could have a credo, too. I could spell out what I believed in a few sentences and use that belief system as the basis for my talks and speeches that would inspire others.

I have a lot of positive thoughts. But where do you begin creating a credo? Begin in a happy place! A cookie is a happy thing but it's small. I have always believed that small bite-sized morsels make the best cookies. What's bigger than a cookie? A watermelon! Ten luscious letters lying idle, waiting on the vine for a mnemonic to come

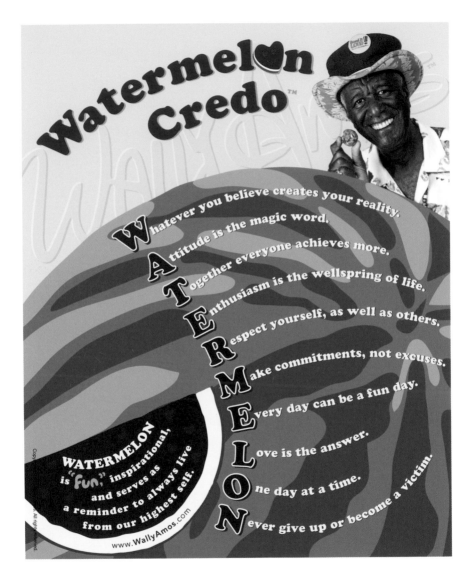

Watermelon Credo™

Whatever you believe creates your reality.

Attitude is the magic word.

Together everyone achieves more.

Enthusiasm is the wellspring of life.

Respect yourself, as well as others.

Make commitments, not excuses.

Every day can be a fun day.

Love is the answer.

One day at a time.

Never give up or become a victim.

WATERMELON is *"fun,"* inspirational, and serves as a reminder to always live from our highest self.

www.WallyAmos.com

along. If you know the meaning of "mnemonic" and can pronounce it and spell it correctly, the next time you see me, I'll give you a cookie.

Anyway, my Watermelon Credo began as a wall poster. It was bright and cheery, like everything is about watermelon, and, like watermelon on a hot summer day, my poster met with a ready reception. People loved it. When I used the Watermelon Credo poster last year in a column I wrote for the *Costco Connection* newsletter, it got a fabulous response. And so I was inspired to elaborate on the original Watermelon Credo poster and come up with *Watermelon Credo – The Book*.

As much as I like to talk about cookies, this book is not about cookies. This book is about my Watermelon Credo. Found in abundance in every part of the world where people love to laugh and eat, watermelon is a natural and nutritious wonder of this universe. I get ecstatic just thinking about the luscious, vine-ripened oblong or globe-shaped object, so gorgeously green on the outside, so brilliantly red on the inside, with its abundantly exuberantly sweet flavor ready and eager to burst out of its perfectly God-made case.

There is the weighty feel of a watermelon, a solid, nearly hollow drum waiting to be thumped. Then there is the ceremony of cutting into it, releasing a tantalizingly sweet aroma, accompanied by the oozing of its remarkable juiciness. Need I say more? Oh yes! After all the thumping, cutting, aroma-inhaling, and juice-letting, there is that extraordinarily satisfying experience of tasting that fructose-laden, flavor-infused fruit flesh. For me, the experience of eating watermelon is a jubilant roller-coaster ride of contrasting colors and textures, capped by sublime flavor.

Watermelon is fun. It's inspirational – even the most enormous watermelon springs from a single seed! – and it serves as a reminder that you are larger than life, and you must always live life from your highest self. You can count the seeds of a watermelon but you can't count the watermelons in a seed. By that,

I mean you shouldn't take things for granted. Marvel at the opportunities and experiences that surround you. Don't let events overwhelm you. You have the power to create and change events by what you believe. Let the Watermelon Credo help you to discover your highest self and to use your inner strength and beauty to make the world a better place.

Please join me as I embark on a trip that follows the tenets of the Watermelon Credo to your inner self. Assimilating this credo will help prepare you for the good times *and* the rough times that lie ahead.

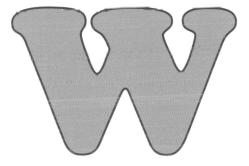

Whatever you believe creates your reality.

Remember the scene in the movie *Dirty Dancing* when the dewy-eyed teen Baby Houseman is led into the staff quarters where heartthrob Johnny Castle is dancing wildly? Hotel guests like Baby aren't allowed to mix socially with the staff, so when Johnny sees her there, he asks his cousin disapprovingly, "What's she doing here?" Baby speaks up meekly, explaining: "I carried a watermelon." That was Baby's reality at a moment when she saw herself as an intruder into the world of dirty dancing. Had she not been so in awe of Johnny, she could have chosen a different reality and said, "I'm here because I'm desperate to break out of the mold my parents have locked me into," or she could have just said, "Johnny, I want to dance like that."

Your belief system is your reality. Why create a reality that you don't like? The words you choose frame your perception of the world. That's why it's so important to choose words that underline the positive aspects of everything you think and say and do.

Thoughts and words have the power to transform. Careless whispers can cause hurt and pain. Once spoken, cruel words cannot be withdrawn. Words chosen with care – words that console and compliment – can heal wounds and

create joy. Like a spoonful of sugar,
sweet words make it easier to drink a
bitter brew. It's so easy to alter
someone else's reality by
helping them refocus their
attitude. You see the world
through a lens. So why not rotate the
lens away from the blur of negativity
Into sharper focus?

    With a change of heart, a change of attitude,
and more carefully chosen words, you can create
a reality that works for you. In you, the world will
become what you think it is.

    Believe that life is a positive experience
and it will be.

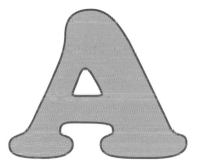

Attitude is the magic word.

The greatest asset you can possess is a positive attitude that springs from your personal belief system. When most people think of "attitude," they think first of that sassy, look-at-me, who-cares-about-you way some people have of presenting themselves.

When most people think of "assets," they think of money and material things. When I think of assets, I think of a positive attitude that reflects a positive outlook.

I wasn't always positive. I was born poor, and many years passed before I realized what valuable assets I had been born with and had had all along. As a young man making my own way in the world, I suffered society-inflicted and self-inflicted wounds that left me with low self-esteem. At the time, we called it an "inferiority complex." Feeling inferior, influenced by what I believed others thought of me, I labeled myself a loser.

Eventually, I developed a belief system of my own that made me believe in myself. I realized I could choose how to feel, how to see myself and define my reality, how to choose a course of action, and ultimately how to create the results in my life.

Nothing good ever comes from being negative. Time and again when faced with personal, financial, and physical challenges, I have found that a positive attitude brings a positive result.

You have the right to choose. Whatever situation befalls you, from your first waking moment to your last day as a thinking, feeling individual on this earth, you can always choose to be positive.

That's why I say, be positive, regardless.

Together everyone achieves more.

One hand can draw a house, but how many hands working together does it take to build a house? In a kung-fu movie, it's hilarious to see the hero surrounded by six or eight vicious villains, menacing him with all manner of weapons greater than his own.

Yet the kung-fu hero always manages to parry each villain's every thrust, vanquishing each in turn, resulting in the bad guys' collective failure. All the while, it's crystal-clear to the viewer that the villains could actually defeat the kung-fu guy if only they worked together: "Hey, guys, on the count of three, let's all get him."

Blockbuster movies and big-league sports require big-time heroes and superstars, who earn millions of dollars, so that fans can ooh and aah and root for their idol to overcome any odds. Even so, in team sports, superstars can't look super or move the ball to the goal unless their team members are working with them. As a high-school basketball player in Hawaii, young Barry Obama liked to showboat his personal style, but the future president of the United States had a lot to learn about what it meant to be on a team. He later admitted. "I learned a lot about discipline, about handling disappointment, being more team-oriented, and realizing not everything is about you."

I've written many times about how I lost control of the original Famous Amos Cookie Company. To succeed, a company needs a management team and a workforce working in concert for the good of the enterprise. I made the mistake of thinking the company was all about me and never realized that I could be part of the problems that befell it. Now I subscribe to the TEAM adage, that Together Everyone Accomplishes More.

This is what I've learned: I am more than I am but far less than we are.

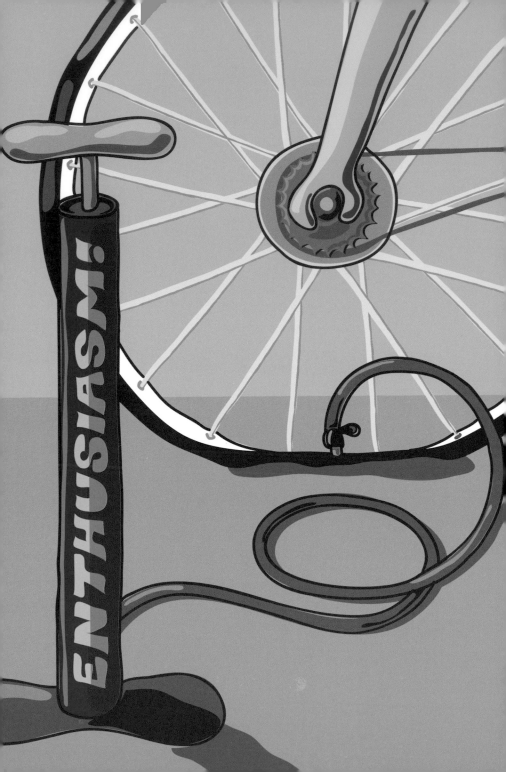

Enthusiasm is the wellspring of life.

I am enthusiastic about what I am doing right now because I choose to live a cheerful, joyful life in the present. Enthusiasm is what gets me going and keeps me going.

By the time I was 30, I had worked my way up

to a good job as a talent agent with the William Morris Agency in New York City. Eager to make it on my own, I quit the agency, and moved to California to work as a personal manager for a single client. A month later, I was jobless, homeless, with a wife and two-month-old son, and my wife, Shirlee, was soon hospitalized. Though I had not yet developed a personal belief system, I knew instinctively that only a positive attitude would lift me above the hardships I faced. Enthusiasm got me through those tough times and inspired me to create Famous Amos, which led me to become the Wally Amos I am today.

If you are enthusiastic about something, it will renew you and make you whole. Being enthusiastic is a choice. It's as easy as rolling out of bed, and what's more, like getting up in the morning, enthusiasm doesn't cost you anything! What a deal! Just pump up some new enthusiasm and there you go: a new you is on the move.

It's different with children. Children are naturally enthusiastic about many things, especially candy, soft drinks, and toys. We have to direct their natural enthusiasm toward the things that will be key to their mental and physical growth, including healthful foods, plenty of exercise, and the thing that I'm most enthusiastic about – reading! It's amazing how much the tiniest of tots can absorb when a story is read aloud. Their little minds leap ahead, storing images, words, and ideas for future use. Reading creates the kind of enthusiasm and joy about learning that can and should last a lifetime.

There is no limit to what can be accomplished with enough enthusiasm.

*I'm enthusiastic about my involvement in the public-private partnership called Read it **LOUD!** It's been shown that reading aloud to little children is the absolute best way to prepare them for learning to read and reading as they grow. Why? Because it's fun; and because it's fun, children are enthusiastic about something that will be so important to their Internet-based future or whatever joyful thing happens next.*

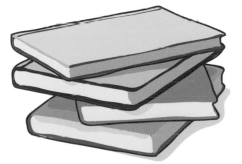

Respect yourself,
as well as others.

When Aretha Franklin wails about needing a little R-E-S-P-E-C-T, she hits a nerve among millions of women, and men too, who moan they are unappreciated by their partners. While you demand respect from others, and it feels good to get it, respect starts at home - with you. Aretha knows that. That's what empowers her to sing that song the way she does.

Your self-image is in your hands. Like a public relations practitioner or a "spin doctor," you create the image others see of you. In essence, you choose what others will see, which in turn determines whether they will respect you.

The amazing Michael Jackson had it right in "Man in the Mirror," when he sang that if we want to make the world a better place, we'd better take a look at ourselves. To change the world, you need to begin by formulating your own belief system. This will make it possible for you to respect the person you see in the mirror and, by extension, respect others who are but a reflection of you.

Look at the people around you. They are just like you. They are made the same way by just like you. They are made the same way by the same creator. Give them their due. Choose to find something praiseworthy in every person you encounter. Why tear anything down when you can help build something better? It's that old Do Unto Others thing.

When you begin to respect yourself, your whole world changes.

Make commitments,
not excuses.

Saying "I might, but then I might not" is an
energy-wasting, lazy way to live your life. It lets you
wobble all over the road, making excuses before
and after the fact for things you wanted to do and
meant to do, but didn't do.

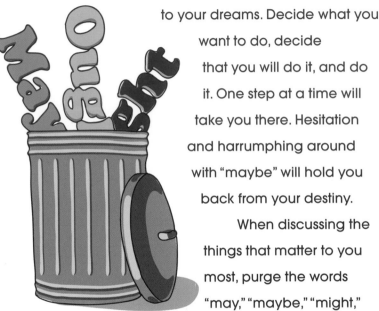

Choosing to say "I will" instead of "I guess," "I hope," or "I'll try," will steer you along the road to your dreams. Decide what you want to do, decide that you will do it, and do it. One step at a time will take you there. Hesitation and harrumphing around with "maybe" will hold you back from your destiny.

When discussing the things that matter to you most, purge the words "may," "maybe," "might," and "ought to" from your vocabulary, and rely on the word "will."

If you know what you want to do, say you "will" do it, tell everyone you "will" do it, and follow up by doing it. Choosing to say "I will" is a positive step. It's the verbal equivalent of turning a key and firing your jets. Go beyond the excuse word "but" – as in I would do it *but* I'm too busy, *but* I'm too young, *but* I'm too old. You'll find that things are brighter on the other side of "but." I thought I was too old *but* discovered I wasn't.

Choose to commit yourself to a course. Let your conviction that you will get it done act as your compass. With the words "I will" keeping you on course, every day at every turn, choose the path that leads to that destination, that dream you've been dreaming.

Use "willpower" not "won't power" to power you to the finish line.

Discover the enormous power in the words "Yes, I will!"

Every day can
be a fun day.

There are easily a million ways to have fun in this world. How many ways can you think of to have fun today? How many reasons can you think of to stop you from having fun?

Whoa, if you thought of 500 ways to have fun

and then came up with 1,000 reasons to stop you, you need an attitude adjustment. Stop what you're thinking. Turn yourself around. Stand on one foot. Stand on your head. Play a kazoo. *Whoo whoo whoo.* Slip outside the office or the house and walk around the block backward. Now start thinking of ways to really have fun.

There's no reason why you can't have fun doing what you're doing. Sure, life gets serious, and you've got responsibilities and bills to pay. Hoohah! Who doesn't? Who says you can't have fun along the way? Remember, it's a long way from Piccadilly to Tipperary, whatever that means. It doesn't really matter what it means if it's fun to say it! Six thick thistle sticks! There. Say that six times.

Fun adds light and lightness to your day. A day without fun is like a day without sunshine. The more you laugh, the easier it is to get things done. Have you heard people say they enjoy their work? Is it because they enjoy *what* they do or they enjoy it *while* they're doing it? Or is it the same thing?

Nearly 50 years ago, author Norman Cousins

documented how watching funny movies and reading funny books cured him of a serious disease. Word of his laughter-as-medicine cure spread, and he reportedly received thousands of letters from doctors who concurred with his self-treatment.

Find ways to put fun into whatever you do. Share your silliest feelings with someone who needs a laugh. Have you noticed that one fun-loving person can walk into a room and remove the doom and gloom? Why not be the person who brings joy to others?

Fun is the lubricant that keeps life moving forward. Laugh a lot.

Love is the answer.

If I ask you to draw a picture of love, what would you draw? Hearts and flowers, those age-old tributes you give to your beloved? Cupid, that cherub of Roman mythology who inspires romantic love by quaintly shooting arrows into unsuspecting hearts? Or a gold wedding band, that circle of eternity? To me, these traditional symbols of love fall short. A concept of love should be infinite, and embrace your children, family members, friends, neighbors, and all there is to love.

Love isn't simple, and learning to love isn't always easy. In my 1988 book *The Power in You*, I explained how hard it was for me to love my mother. As a child, I heard a lot about love in church, but at home I got whipped a lot. Years later, I came to understand that it's impossible to love others if you sit in judgment of them. Finally, I was able to accept and love my mother as she was.

I discovered that love is not like physics, calculus, or cake: the more love you give away, the more love you have.

Living in Hawaii for many years, I have come to believe that the Hawaiians have the right idea about aloha, their word for love. There are 39 definitions of "aloha" in the Hawaiian dictionary. Apart from being the word for hello and goodbye, aloha is the word for love, affection, compassion, mercy, sympathy, and kindness, to name but a few. According to traditional lore, aloha embodies positive values like unity, humility, patience, and understanding, expressed with tenderness, harmony, pleasantness, modesty, and perseverance. What an ideal way to regard love, an emotion that is as wide as the ocean, that goes out to others when we greet them and bid them farewell.

For more than 300 years, a horizontal figure eight as a never-ending ribbon has symbolized the mathematical and philosophical concept of infinity. Imagine yourself as one half of this figure. The other half is everything else there is for you to embrace with compassion, to appreciate with understanding, and ultimately to love.

Love is the greatest force in the universe.

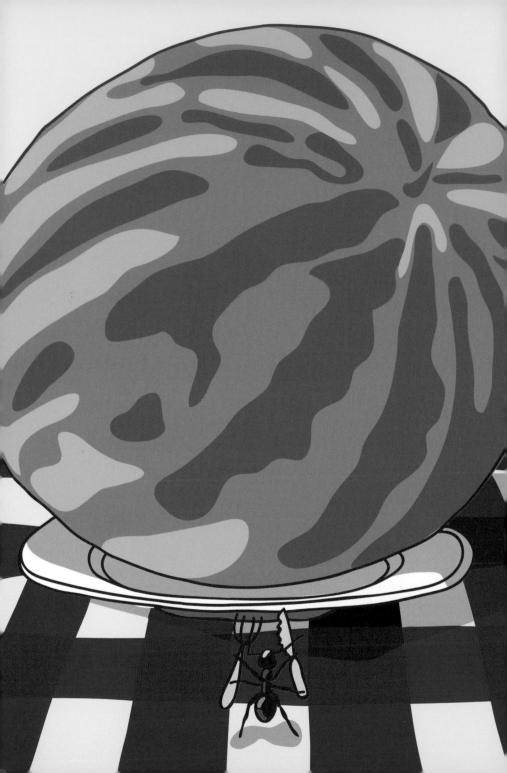

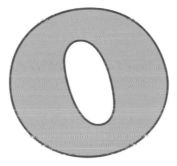

One day at a time.

How do you eat an elephant? (If you're a vegetarian, imagine a watermelon the size of an elephant. The answer is the same.) One bite at a time.

Life is not lived in a lump. It is lived moment

by moment. What you choose to do with each moment is up to you. But just as ancient Chinese philosopher Lao Tse noted in the *Tao-Te Ching*, even the longest journey begins with the first step. The phrase taking life "one step at a time" isn't just a metaphor; it is the way of life.

Many of us spend our lives planning for our future. From youth through our years as adults, we are constantly trying to decide what we will be when we grow up, and as grown-ups we are planning our retirement. But life, like time itself, is a continuum. It is all one, and it is now.

Years ago, upon awaking from a nap on a long flight from Hawaii to the mainland, my daughter Sarah asked, "Are we here yet?" In fact, we are always here. We are never "there," and we never live in the past or the future. It's important to live in the moment, and be all that we can be at that moment in time.

The only way to live is one day at a time. What we choose to do with our time may make time seem heavy on our hands, passing slowly, or make us feel that time is flying past, leaving not enough hours in a day to accomplish all that we want to do. But the notion of time passing fast or slow is an illusion.

Live according to your own belief system, and avoid the temptation to regret actions in the past or to try to plan the future. Focus on what was positive in past years, and don't worry about the future, which can never be what we imagine it will be. Undertake every day and every project bit by bit, moving forward from inception through completion but never more than one bit at a time.

All of life happens in increments, one at a time.

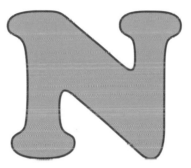

Never give up or become a victim.

If you give up, you are guaranteed to lose. If you let yourself be victimized, you are guaranteed to be a victim.

At the outset of the Second World War in Europe, when other countries were falling to Hitler's armies, Winston Churchill advised Britons, "Never, never, never give up."

Growing up in this country, we get a lot of advice about holding our moral ground when we know we are right: Stand firm, stand pat, stay the course, stick it out, stick to your guns.

If you're a Western music fan, you know Tammy Wynette was proud and resolute when she vowed to "Stand by Her Man," and if you're a fan of classic R&B songs, you know that Ben E. King was emboldened to go on through the darkness of night and sidestep mountains tumbling to the sea when he sang of his friend's stick-to-itiveness in "Stand by Me."

Once I learned the word stick-to-itiveness, I got stuck on it. And once you determine for yourself what is right for you, you should not let anyone stick it to you.

Stand up for what you believe in, and for what you believe is right. Stand up against injustice. Take a stand. Stand up for change. And keep at it.

You no doubt remember how Dr. Seuss told a tale of peculiar persistence in the ever-amusing and always rhyming verses of *Green Eggs and Ham*. A pair of characters are unrelenting in their determination not to yield to the other's wishes. Sam-I-Am is doggedly intent on getting his friend to taste green eggs and ham. And his friend is equally obstinate in his refusal to try the dish. Of course, when the friend finally discovers he loves the taste of ham topped with green eggs, he praises Sam for his perseverance.

Perseverance pays. Remember, a diamond was once just a dirty piece of coal that stuck to its job.

Toward a More Watermelony World

Watermelon was a comfort food for me years before I tasted home-baked chocolate-chip cookies for the first time. (Thank you, Aunt Della!)

I was born in Tallahassee, Florida, in the years before Americans began to make good on the promise of racial equality. Ignoring the guarantees of the U.S. Constitution, Jim Crow laws of the period made it possible for one group of Americans to denigrate and discriminate against another group of American citizens solely because of the color of their skin.

Everyone I knew in the colored section of Tallahassee loved watermelon, but we all knew it was shameful for blacks to be seen eating watermelon in public, and nobody knew why. It seems that the opprobrium regarding blacks and watermelons dates back to a time when ex-slaves were seen eating watermelon on rural roadsides while polite white society ate their watermelon off plates in the parlor or out of picnic hampers in the park. The noted East Coast printmakers Currier & Ives depicted these roadside sights in the 1880s, and the early twentieth century *Our Gang* film comedies carried them forward.

In *Watermelon Magic: Seeds of Wisdom, Slices of Life*, I set out to explain that it is okay for anyone who loves watermelon to eat watermelon, privately or publicly. The premise of *Watermelon Magic* is that you may make your own decisions based on your personal preferences and what you believe. It is not all right for other people to tell you what is right for you. It is not all right for you to be duped by stereotypes circulated by racists and bigots for the purpose of oppressing people of other races, religions, and cultures.

If you are shocked to learn that only 50 years ago it was considered a no-no for African Americans to eat watermelon in public, it may be even more shocking for you to learn that to this day, there are educators who think my Watermelon Credo poster is offensive, probably for related reasons. People are still influenced by vicious and nonsensical stereotypes that have been circulating for who knows how long.

I was reminded of this unfortunate attitude when a teacher in New Jersey told me her vice principal had removed the Watermelon Credo poster from a classroom wall. Let me summarize my credo again: I believe that every human being can choose to lead a life of happiness and joy. No one can tell you what you can eat or what you should believe. No matter who you are or what you've been through, you can create your own belief system and live an inspiring life.

Many educators have responded to the Watermelon Credo poster by requesting copies for their classrooms. This interest was definitely one thing that inspired me to write the Watermelon Credo book. I feel pleased and honored to be able to have the opportunity to positively impact the lives of young people.

My credo has become a map that guides me through my daily routines. It's the thing I go to when I need that extra assurance or reminder that I am on the right path. It helps me remember past experiences and what it took to get me through. Just as the Watermelon Credo helps me navigate my life's journey, creating your own personal credo might do the same for you. You can choose your own personal object, no matter what it is, and write your own inspiring principles to go with its letters. Then use your credo on a daily basis. It will make your travels through life a whole lot easier. Try it. You have nothing to lose and everything to gain.

A watermelon begins with a single seed. Take that to heart and grow your own future.

About Wally Amos

Wally Amos is a famous name throughout the world. As founder of the Famous Amos Chocolate Chip Cookie Company in 1975, he was the father of the modern gourmet chocolate-chip cookie industry. His most recent business venture is Chip & Cookie®, a chain of retail cookie stores in Hawaii, where he bakes his "original recipe" chocolate chip cookies that are acclaimed as "America's Best Tasting Cookies"® and also sells Chip & Cookie character dolls, along with apparel, books, and other gift items. In 1992, he helped form the Uncle Wally's® Muffin Company, which produces an extensive line of gourmet ready-to-eat muffins.

Wally is a sought-after motivational speaker who spends much of his time supporting educational causes. He was National Spokesman for Literacy Volunteers of America from 1979 until 2002, when they merged with Laubach Literacy International to create ProLiteracy Worldwide. As an early childhood literacy advocate, Wally founded and is chairman of the board of the Read it **LOUD!** Foundation, an organization that encourages parents to read aloud to their children for 10 minutes a day from birth through age six. He has also served on the boards of the National Center for Family Literacy and Communities in Schools.

A humble, happy man with a big heart, Wally gave the shirt off his back and the battered Panama hat off his head to the Smithsonian Institution's Warshaw Collection of Business Americana, where the shirt and hat are on display. He has been inducted into the Babson College Entrepreneurs Hall of Fame, and has been the recipient of the Horatio Alger Award, the President's Award for Entrepreneurial Excellence, and the National Literacy Honors Award.

In addition to appearing on the cover of *TIME* magazine, Wally has appeared in numerous TV sitcoms and been profiled in countless television and radio shows and in newspaper and magazine feature stories. On the lecture circuit, he regularly addresses corporate and educational groups worldwide with his inspiring philosophy, "Be positive regardless!"

For more information on Wally, visit these Web sites: chipandcookie.com, unclewallys.com, and readitloud.org, as well as the Apple Apps Work link: soundmarketingapps.com/positive/support.html.

More Books by Wally Amos

The Famous Amos Story: The Face That Launched a Thousand Chips. This book details the trials and tribulations that went into creating the Famous Amos Cookie Company, the first cookie boutique to do more than a million dollars a year in sales. His first cookie store in Hollywood brought Wally fame and fortune but not the happiness and inner peace it would take him years to find. Written with Leroy Robinson (Doubleday, New York, 1983).

The Power in You: Ten Secret Ingredients for Inner Strength. This remarkable work of self–help and inspiration, filled with personal insights, reveals 10 secret ingredients that combine to create a life of personal satisfaction and love. Written with his son, Gregory Amos (Donald I. Fine/Penguin, New York, 1988).

Man with No Name: Turn Lemons Into Lemonade. This story tells how Wally founded the Famous Amos Cookie Company and lost everything, including use of his name. Dr. Deepak Chopra says this book shows us how to find the seeds of greatness in adversity. Written with Camilla Denton (Aslan, Lower Lake, California, 1994).

Watermelon Magic: Seeds of Wisdom, Slices of Life. Witty and amusing, this book is about changing and growing, and making healthy choices for yourself. Written with Stu Glauberman (Beyond Words, Hillsboro, Oregon, 1996).

The Cookie Never Crumbles: Inspirational Recipes for Everyday Living. Wally writes about how you can be happy, no matter what befalls you. Poet Maya Angelou thanked Wally for putting his wise words onto these pages. Written with Eden–Lee Murray (St. Martin's Griffin, New York, 2001).

Be Positive! Be Positive! Insights on How to Live an Inspiring and Joy–Filled Life. Wally offers experience–based insights into the value of persistence and perseverance for overcoming challenges and achieving a positive outlook (Blue Mountain, Boulder, Colorado, 2006).

The Power of Self-Esteem: How to Discover and Fulfill Your Life Dreams. Years of thinking and writing about self–esteem prompted Wally to offer advice on how to dream, place a high value on one's self and learn from past mistakes. Written with Stu Glauberman (Blue Mountain, Boulder, Colorado, 2006).

Live an Inspiring Life: 10 Secret Ingredients for Inner Strength. A chip off his major work, *The Power in You,* this book redefines the ingredients that go into Wally's recipe for inner strength. Learn how to combine them to live a joyous, fun, and inspiring life. Written with Stu Glauberman (Blue Mountain, Boulder, Colorado, 2006).

The Path to Success is Paved with Positive Thinking: How to Live a Joy-Filled Life and Make Your Dreams Come True. Full of Wally's witty and wise lessons, this book is a how–to guide for achieving your fullest potential. Written with Stu Glauberman (Blue Mountain, Boulder, Colorado, 2008).

Wally Amos's books can be
purchased directly from him at:
Credo Press™
PO Box 897
Kailua, HI 96734
tel. 808.261.1811
Books can also be purchased at www.chipandcookie.com.